Congressional
Research
Service

Climate Change and Existing Law: A Survey of Legal Issues Past, Present, and Future

Robert Meltz
Legislative Attorney

July 23, 2012

Congressional Research Service
7-5700
www.crs.gov
R42613

CRS Report for Congress
Prepared for Members and Committees of Congress

Summary

This report surveys *existing* law for legal issues that have arisen, or may arise in the future, on account of climate change and government responses thereto.

At the threshold of many climate-change-related lawsuits are two barriers—whether the plaintiff has standing to sue and whether the claim being made presents a political question. Both barriers have forced courts to apply amorphous standards in a new and complex context.

Efforts to mitigate climate change—that is, reduce greenhouse gas (GHG) emissions—have spawned a host of legal issues. The Supreme Court resolved a big one in 2007—the Clean Air Act (CAA), it said, does authorize EPA to regulate GHG emissions. Quite recently, a host of issues raised by EPA's efforts to carry out that authority were resolved in the agency's favor by the D.C. Circuit. Another issue is whether EPA's "endangerment finding" for GHG emissions from new motor vehicles will compel EPA to move against GHG emissions under other CAA authorities. Still other mitigation issues are (1) the role of the Endangered Species Act in addressing climate change; (2) how climate change must be considered under the National Environmental Policy Act; (3) liability and other questions raised by carbon capture and sequestration; (4) constitutional constraints on land use regulation and state actions against climate change; and (5) whether the public trust doctrine applies to the atmosphere.

Liability for harms allegedly caused by climate change has raised another crop of legal issues. The Supreme Court decision that the CAA bars federal judges from imposing their own limits on GHG emissions from power plants has led observers to ask: Can plaintiffs alleging climate change harms still seek monetary damages, and are state law claims still allowed? The one ruling so far says no to both. Questions of insurance policy coverage are also likely to be litigated. Finally, the applicability of international law principles to climate change has yet to be resolved.

Water shortages thought to be induced by climate change likely will lead to litigation over the nature of water rights. Shortages have already prompted several lawsuits over whether cutbacks in water delivered from federal projects effect Fifth Amendment takings or breaches of contract.

Sea level rise and extreme precipitation linked to climate change raise questions as to (1) the effect of sea level rise on the beachfront owner's property line; (2) whether public beach access easements migrate with the landward movement of beaches; (3) design and operation of federal levees; and (4) government failure to take preventive measures against climate change harms.

Other adaptation responses to climate change raising legal issues, often property rights related, are beach armoring (seawalls, bulkheads, etc.), beach renourishment, and "retreat" measures. Retreat measures seek to move existing development away from areas likely to be affected by floods and sea level rise, and to discourage new development there.

Natural disasters to which climate change contributes may prompt questions as to whether response actions taken in an emergency are subject to relaxed requirements and, similarly, as to the rebuilding of structures destroyed by such disasters just as they were before.

Finally, immigration and refugee law appear not to cover persons forced to relocate because of climate change impacts such as drought or sea level rise.

Contents

Contacts

T his report surveys *existing* law for legal issues that have arisen, or may arise in the future, on account of climate change and government responses thereto. The reader interested in proposals for *new* laws to deal with climate change is referred to other works.[1] Of course, while this report covers many of the major legal issues that have emerged or may do so, the endless ramifications of climate change preclude any claim to exhaustiveness.

The report takes as its point of departure the current scientific consensus that climate change is occurring and, to the degree it continues, will cause sea level rise and extreme weather events.[2] Inclusion of some legal issues was based further on the predominant scientific view that human activities are contributing to climate change.[3]

Finally, it should be noted that the discussion of several topics in this report likely would have to be substantially modified, or possibly deleted, if Congress were to enact comprehensive climate change legislation. Such legislation might limit or displace the role of certain existing statutes— the Clean Air Act and the Endangered Species Act being prime candidates—or common law in addressing climate change.

I. Threshold Barriers to Litigation

Federal courts have evolved a variety of gatekeeper doctrines to ensure that only certain plaintiffs and certain types of claims can invoke their jurisdiction. Two of these doctrines, standing and political question, have posed daunting barriers for plaintiffs in climate change cases.

Standing doctrine. This principle flows from Article III of the Constitution, which limits the jurisdiction of courts created under that article (such as federal district courts) to "cases" or "controversies." These words are construed to require a person who sues in an Article III court to show (1) "injury in fact" (existing or imminent), (2) "causation" (described as a fairly traceable connection between the injury in fact and the defendant's conduct), and (3) "redressability" (meaning that plaintiff's injury is likely to be remedied by the relief plaintiff seeks).[4] A plaintiff not satisfying any of these elements is said to lack standing; his or her suit will be dismissed.

It should be apparent that a plaintiff complaining of injury from climate change may be thwarted by any of the three standing requirements. For example, how does such a plaintiff show the second element, causation? How does he show, say, that a drought that destroyed his crops was caused by climate change—indeed, by climate change to which the defendant's greenhouse gas (GHG) emissions contributed?[5] To be sure, in two climate change decisions, *Massachusetts v.*

---

[1] *See, e.g.,* Michael B. Gerrard (ed.), GLOBAL CLIMATE CHANGE AND U.S. LAW (American Bar Ass'n 2007); Tom Mounteer (ed.), CLIMATE CHANGE DESKBOOK (Envtl. Law Inst. 2009); CRS Report R40556, *Market-Based Greenhouse Gas Control Selected Proposals in the 111th Congress,* by Larry Parker, Brent D. Yacobucci, and Jonathan L. Ramseur.

[2] National Research Council, ADVANCING THE SCIENCE OF CLIMATE CHANGE 2 (2010). *See generally* CRS Report RL33849, *Climate Change Science and Policy Implications,* by Jane A. Leggett.

[3] National Research Council, *supra* note 2, at 2.

[4] *See, e.g.,* Lujan v. Defenders of Wildlife, 504 U.S. 555, 560 (1992).

[5] *See, e.g.,* Native Village of Kivalina v. ExxonMobil Corp., 663 F. Supp. 2d 863, 880 (N.D. Cal. 2009) ("there is no realistic possibility of tracing any particular alleged effect of global warming to any particular emissions by any specific person ..."), *appeal pending before Ninth Circuit.*

EPA in the Supreme Court[6] and *American Elec. Power Co. v. Connecticut* in the Second Circuit,[7] Article III standing was found—but specifically for *state* plaintiffs.[8] *Massachusetts* asserted that states are entitled to "special solicitude" when seeking to establish standing,[9] and both decisions noted the sovereign status of states as *parens patriae* (literally, father of the country).[10] Case law since these decisions, however, has rejected their extension to private plaintiffs, who have often encountered difficulty establishing standing in climate change cases.[11] True, such plaintiffs may seek to avoid Article III standing issues by attempting to establish standing in state courts. But if, as is likely, the lawsuit takes aim at GHG emissions from out-of-state sources, the defendants are likely to remove the case to federal court under federal question or diversity jurisdiction. Thus the question of Article III standing likely will need to be faced.

A specialized issue is whether Indian tribes, by virtue of their inherent sovereignty, should also be able to establish standing through *parens patriae* status.[12] The argument for tribal *parens patriae* standing was rejected by the district court in *Native Village of Kivalina v. ExxonMobil Corp.*, a case in which an Eskimo village seeks damages for coastal erosion allegedly caused by climate change to which the defendants' GHG emissions assertedly contribute.[13] The case is now on appeal to the Ninth Circuit.

Political question doctrine. While standing asks whether there is a proper *plaintiff* before the court, political question doctrine asks whether there is a justiciable *claim*. The doctrine seeks to restrain courts from inappropriate interference in the business of the other branches of government—often because resolving the issue necessarily involves policy determinations. Six factors indicating a non-justiciable political question (any one of which may be dispositive) were famously stated by the Supreme Court in *Baker v. Carr* in 1962.[14] Of these, the first three have played a role in the climate-change nuisance cases:

> a textually demonstrable constitutional commitment of the issue to a coordinate political department; or a lack of judicially discoverable and manageable standards for resolving it; or

---

[6] 549 U.S. 497 (2007).

[7] 582 F.3d 309 (2d Cir. 2009), *reversed on other grounds*, 131 S. Ct. 2527 (2011) (affirming the Second Circuit's finding of standing by equally divided vote).

[8] *See generally* Kirsten Engle, *State Standing in Climate Change Lawsuits*, 26 J. Land Use & Envtl. L. 217 (2011).

[9] 549 U.S. at 520.

[10] *Massachusetts*, 549 U.S. at 518-520; Connecticut v. American Elec. Power Co., 582 F.3d 309, 338-339 (2d Cir. 2009), *reversed on other grounds*, 131 S. Ct. 2527 (2011). That is, Article III is satisfied when a state brings suit as *parens patriae* on behalf of its citizens. *Massachusetts*, 549 U.S. at 519-521.

Parens patriae doctrine allows a state to sue in its sovereign capacity to protect its citizenry, rather than being limited, as Article III would normally require, to asserting traditional particularized injuries to state interests. The modern origins of the doctrine lie in two century-old nuisance cases brought by states in federal court alleging interstate pollution: *Missouri v. Illinois*, 180 U.S. 208 (1901), and *Georgia v. Tennessee Copper Co*, 206 U.S. 230 (1907). In both cases, state standing was found. The current test for *parens patriae* standing is found in *Snapp & Son, Inc. v. Puerto Rico*, 458 U.S. 592 (1982), though there is some question whether traditional Article III standing requirements have to be met as well by the citizens of the state asserting *parens patriae* standing.

[11] *See, e.g.*, Comer v. Murphy Oil USA, Inc., 2012 Westlaw 933670 (S.D. Miss. March 20, 2012) (finding of Article III standing for state sovereign in *Massachusetts v. EPA* does not support standing for private plaintiffs here); *Native Village of Kivalina*, 663 F. Supp. 2d at 882 (same).

[12] *See generally* Elizabeth Ann Kronk, *Effective Access to Justice Applying the Parens Patriae Standing Doctrine to Climate Change-Related Claims Brought by Native Nations*, 32 Pub. Land & Res. L. Rev. 1 (2011).

[13] 663 F. Supp. 2d 863 (N.D. Cal. 2009).

[14] 369 U.S. 186, 216 (1962).

the impossibility of deciding [the issue] without an initial policy determination of a kind clearly for nonjudicial discretion....

Baker made clear it was setting a high threshold for nonjusticiability; since it was decided a half-century ago, the Court has found few issues to present political questions. But the doctrine has been ubiquitous in the nuisance-based climate change litigation with more courts rejecting such claims on that ground than not.[15]

Addendum. At this point, the reader is referred to Section III.A., "A. Liability After *American Electric Power Co., Inc. v. Connecticut*," which discusses yet another litigation barrier: federal displacement of common-law-based climate change claims by the Clean Air Act. This barrier, where it applies, makes it unnecessary for courts to reach the standing and political question issues in the case, and thus allows them to avoid the abstruse questions raised by those defenses.

II. Mitigation—Reducing GHG Emissions

Proactive responses to climate change are usually grouped under one of two headings: mitigation and adaptation. This section treats some of the legal issues raised by mitigation. Sections IV and V compile some of the legal issues associated with adaptation.

A. *Massachusetts v. EPA* and EPA's GHG Rules Under the Clean Air Act

In 2007, the Supreme Court answered a fundamental Clean Air Act (CAA) question. The act, it found in *Massachusetts v. EPA*,[16] gives EPA authority to regulate GHG emissions. Such authority is granted, said the Court, because the CAA term "air pollutant" is defined sufficiently broadly in the act to include GHGs. Moreover, the Court added, the CAA forecloses an EPA decision not to regulate GHGs or any other air pollutant simply because the administration in power may have policy qualms—for example, due to a preference for non-regulatory approaches. In light of these determinations, the Court instructed EPA to reconsider its 2003 denial of a petition asking it to regulate GHG emissions from new motor vehicles, a denial EPA had based on the Court-rejected reasons.

Following this seminal decision, EPA set about the task of adapting the CAA to address climate change. In doing so, the agency confronted a statute more comfortably suited to regional air pollution problems, the opposite of climate change with its global nature. Four EPA actions in that effort are, in chronological order—

---

[15] Two decisions rejecting common-law claims based on climate-change harms, on political question grounds, are *Native Village of Kivalina*, 63 F. Supp. 2d at 871-877, and *Comer*, 2012 Westlaw 933670 *11-14. Both decisions based their rejection of the claims on the second and third *Baker* factors noted in the text. Declining to accept a political question defense for such claims is *American Electric Power v. Connecticut*, 582 F.3d 309, 323-332 (2d Cir. 2009), *reversed on other grounds*, 131 S. Ct. 2527 (2011). In contrast, no difference of judicial opinion exists when a climate change claim is based on EPA's failure to satisfy requirements in a *statute*, such as the Clean Air Act. There, the claim avoids the absence of clear standards in the common law cases and dismissal on political question grounds is deemed inappropriate. *See, e.g., Massachusetts*, 549 U.S. at 516 (proper construction of a congressional statute, here the Clean Air Act, is a question "eminently suitable to resolution in a federal court").

[16] 549 U.S. 497 (2007).

- **The "timing rule."** This "rule" is actually an EPA memorandum, first issued in 2008. 73 Fed. Reg. 80,300 (2008). The memorandum narrowly interprets the CAA phrase "pollutant subject to regulation under this act"[17] to include only pollutants regulated by *actual, not potential future*, emission limits. To explain, in Prevention of Significant Deterioration (PSD) areas—areas that are cleaner than national standards require—the CAA requires only a "pollutant subject to regulation under this act" to be controlled by potentially expensive "best available control technology" (BACT).[18] Since there were no "actual" GHG regulations under the CAA when the memorandum was issued, this meant that for a while at least, new major emitting facilities in PSD areas did not have to install BACT for GHG emissions. In 2010, EPA reiterated its "actual, not potential future" interpretation, and made clear that even under that view, PSD requirements would kick in on January 2, 2011, when the "tailpipe rule" (below) took effect. 75 Fed. Reg. 17,004 (2010).

- **The "endangerment finding."** 74 Fed. Reg. 66,496 (2009). In this rule, EPA determined that GHG emissions from new motor vehicles "cause, or contribute to, air pollution which may reasonably be anticipated to endanger public health or welfare," per CAA section 202(a)(1). This was pursuant to the reconsideration of the Section 202 petition ordered in Massachusetts. The finding has no effect on outside parties in itself; its importance is that it triggers a duty under CAA Section 202(a) for EPA to promulgate emission standards for new motor vehicles—see immediately below.

- **The "tailpipe rule."** 75 Fed. Reg. 25,323 (2010). In this rule, EPA and the National Highway Traffic Safety Administration set, respectively, GHG emission standards and fuel economy standards for 2012-2016 model year light-duty vehicles.

- **The "tailoring rule."** 75 Fed. Reg. 31,514 (2010). This rule is to relieve the overwhelming permitting burdens that EPA asserts would, in the absence of the rule, fall on PSD and Title V permitting authorities beginning January 2, 2011, when EPA's tailpipe rule took effect. When that happened, the PSD part of the CAA requires by its terms that PSD permits be issued (and BACT applied) for every new major emitting facility in the PSD area that emits more than either 100 or 250 tons of GHGs annually, depending on the source. This is a huge number of sources, so the tailoring rule sets much higher tonnage thresholds for 2011, gradually diminishing, EPA hopes, in following years. That way, EPA expects, federal and state permitters will have time to develop routines for processing the extremely large number of permit applications.

Ninety-five petitions for review challenging these EPA actions, plus EPA's historic interpretation of the PSD section of the CAA, were filed in the D.C. Circuit. A marathon two days of oral argument before the court ensued. On June 26, 2012, the court handed EPA a resounding victory, unanimously upholding in firm language all four of EPA's actions.[19] Briefly, the court held that EPA's endangerment finding is adequately supported by the administrative record. The tailpipe

---

[17] CAA §165(a)(4); 42 U.S.C. §7475(a)(4).

[18] *Id.*

[19] Coalition for Responsible Regulation, Inc. v. EPA, 2012 Westlaw 2381955 (D.C. Cir. June 26, 2012).

rule, it said, is supported by the CAA's plain text and need not consider the rule's consequences for stationary sources of emissions. Turning to the stationary source regulations—the timing rule and tailoring rule—the court first found the PSD portion of the act to cover GHGs. The court then held it could not reach the merits of the rule challenges because petitioners lacked standing in light of their failure to show injury from the rules. For example, the tailoring rule produced a benefit for petitioners, not an injury, since without the rule an even *greater* number of sources would be subject to PSD and Title V permitting.

Assuming, as most observers do, that reversal on further review is unlikely, the D.C. Circuit ruling means at least two things. First, other adjudicative and administrative efforts involving GHG emissions regulation can now proceed. For example, with the endangerment finding under Section 202 now upheld, any EPA endangerment finding under Section 111,[20] governing new source performance standards for stationary sources, will be on firmer ground. That removes a stumbling block to EPA development of new source performance standards for GHG emissions from stationary source categories, such as those currently being finalized under court settlement for fossil-fuel-fired power plants and petroleum refineries.[21] Second, with the judicial option likely closed, states and industries opposed to EPA's efforts to address climate change through the CAA have few options left other than pressing Congress to curtail or eliminate EPA's CAA authority to deal with GHG emissions.

B. Legal Consequences of EPA's Endangerment Finding

With EPA's endangerment finding for new motor vehicle GHG emissions likely having survived judicial challenge, one question comes to the fore: does the finding, made under CAA Section 202, legally compel the agency to make endangerment findings for GHG emissions under other sections of the act that use similar endangerment language for other emission sources? Such subsequent endangerment findings would require, or at least authorize, EPA to regulate GHG emissions under those sections. CRS has explored this question in a separate report.[22] Briefly, that report concludes as follows:

First, the CAA section most likely to require EPA regulatory action after the Section 202 endangerment finding is Section 111. Section 111 requires EPA to set performance standards for those categories of new stationary sources of emissions that "cause, or contribute significantly to, air pollution which may reasonably be anticipated to endanger public health or welfare." The word "significantly," not present in Section 202, suggests that any legal compulsion created by the Section 202 endangerment finding might be limited to those new-source categories with the most prodigious GHG emissions. Section 111, however, affords EPA wide discretion in setting new source performance standards. As Section II.A. notes, EPA has already moved to use Section 111 against GHG emissions, pursuant to litigation settlements.

Second, two other CAA provisions that might be triggered by the Section 202 endangerment finding are Section 108,[23] requiring national ambient air quality standards, and Section 115,[24]

---

[20] 42 U.S.C. §7411.

[21] *See* 77 Fed. Reg. 22392 (April 13, 2012) (proposed standards).

[22] CRS Report R40984, *Legal Consequences of EPA's Endangerment Finding for New Motor Vehicle Greenhouse Gas Emissions*, by Robert Meltz.

[23] 42 U.S.C. §7408.

[24] 42 U.S.C. §7415.

which requires states to revise their implementation plans to prevent or eliminate the endangerment of public health or welfare in a foreign country. As to these sections, however, the arguable infeasibility of achieving the regulatory goals—even if GHG emissions in the United States are significantly reduced, atmospheric concentrations would decline little—may give EPA room to argue that regulatory action is not mandatory. Other endangerment-triggered sections of the CAA can be distinguished from Section 202(a) by their explicit terms, and so likely would not be triggered by the 202(a) endangerment finding—or at least do not impose on EPA a *mandatory* duty to promulgate GHG emission limits.

C. Use of the Endangered Species Act to Restrict GHG Emissions[25]

Some cast the Endangered Species Act (ESA) as a tool aggressive environmental groups may use to thwart projects that produce GHGs. Under this view, plaintiffs would claim that a project's GHG emissions, by contributing to climate change that brings about adverse habitat change, are causing a "take" of protected species in violation of the ESA.[26] For example, a suit could claim that any project that contributes to warmer seas harms, hence "takes," certain listed coral species. However, no case law can be found on this legal argument, either accepting or rejecting it.

Instead of alleging takes of species, lawsuits connecting the ESA to climate change typically are based on how an agency considered climate change when making other determinations: listing a species;[27] designating critical habitat;[28] or issuing a Biological Opinion.[29] The ESA requires that the Fish & Wildlife Service (FWS) consider the effects on habitat, at least in part, for all of those determinations.[30] Accordingly, climate change evaluations long have been part of ESA decision-making, but only to the extent that the climate's effects on habitat are linked to a species.

Case law does not show that the ESA is used as an enforcement tool to make climate change arguments. In the handful of cases where ESA challenges were directed at federal projects related to power plants, only one involved climate change allegations, *Palm Beach County*

---

[25] This section of the report was written by Kristina Alexander, Legislative Attorney, CRS American Law Division.

[26] Habitat change can constitute a "take" of listed species as follows. Under the ESA, "take" is defined as "to harass, harm, pursue, hunt, shoot, wound, kill, trap, capture, or collect, or to attempt to engage in any such conduct." 16 U.S.C. §1532(19). "Harm" in this definition has been defined by the Fish & Wildlife Service to include "significant habitat modification or degradation where it actually kills or injures wildlife." 50 C.F.R. §17.3.

[27] *See, e.g.*, Greater Yellowstone Coalition, Inc. v. Servheen, 665 F.3d 1015 (9th Cir. 2011); In re Polar Bear Endangered Species Act Listing, 794 F. Supp. 2d 65 (D.D.C. 2011); Center for Biological Diversity v. Lubchenco, 758 F. Supp. 2d 945 (N.D. Cal. 2010).

[28] *See, e.g.*, Conservancy of Southwest Florida v. U.S. Fish and Wildlife Service, 2011 WL 1326805 (M.D. Fla. April 06, 2011); Alliance for Wild Rockies v. Lyder, 728 F. Supp. 2d 1126 (D. Mont. 2010).

[29] *See, e.g.*, Center for Biological Diversity v. Salazar, 804 F. Supp. 2d 987 (D. Ariz. 2011); South Yuba River Citizens League v. National Marine Fisheries Service, 723 F. Supp. 2d 1247 (E.D. Cal. 2010); and Pacific Coast Federation of Fishermen's Associations v. Gutierrez, 606 F. Supp. 2d 1122 (E.D. Cal. 2008).

[30] *See* ESA §4(a)(1)(A), 16 U.S.C. §1533(a)(1)(A) (when making determination on whether to list a species, relevant wildlife agency must consider "the present or threatened destruction, modification, or curtailment of its habitat or range"); ESA §4(b)(2), 16 U.S.C. §1533(b)(2) (requiring relevant wildlife agency to designate critical habitat); and ESA §7(a)(2), 16 U.S.C. §1536(a)(2) (requiring all agencies to consult with relevant wildlife agency to determine whether their actions would "result in the destruction or adverse modification of habitat of such species which is determined ... to be critical").

Environmental Coalition v. Florida, and it was not clear whether those claims were premised on the ESA or on another legal basis.[31]

Despite the apparent lack of litigation premised on climate change *taking* species, some regulatory changes were made to limit lawsuits based on that cause of action. In 2008, FWS changed the regulations that dictated how a service considered impacts of federal projects on listed species.[32] Those regulations were effective only from January 15, 2008, to May 5, 2008, after Congress acted to halt them in P.L. 111-8.[33] During that period of regulatory change, definitions related to the effects of an agency action were modified to "reinforce the Services' current view that there is no requirement to consult on [greenhouse gas] emissions' contribution to global warming and its associated impacts on listed species."[34] Despite the revocation of those changes, it does not appear that the scope of effects has expanded, likely due to the fact that the regulations already limited review to those effects with a reasonable certainty to occur.[35]

Another regulatory change of the same time period is still in place. It restricts lawsuits claiming incidental takes of polar bears to instances where the agency action occurs in the state of Alaska.[36]

D. Government Restrictions on Private Activities That Generate GHGs or Reduce Carbon Sinks as Possible Takings of Private Property

Government restrictions on the use of private land always raise the prospect of landowners filing regulatory takings claims under the Fifth Amendment Takings Clause,[37] if such restrictions eliminate much of the land's value. Thus, government prohibition of, say, building a coal-fired power plant on GHG-emitting grounds may generate a takings challenge if the proposed project site is substantially devalued thereby. Research fails to reveal any court decisions in this category, but it can be said that regulatory takings claims in general are rarely successful, usually because other economic use of the site can be made.

Development restrictions on privately owned forests and wetlands on the basis of their carbon-sink value may also give rise to takings claims. A carbon sink is a natural or artificial reservoir that stores some carbon-containing compound. While the oceans are by far the largest carbon

---

[31] Palm Beach County Environmental Coalition v. Florida, 651 F. Supp. 2d 1328 (S.D. Fla. 2009). Plaintiffs also had alleged violations of the Clean Air Act, National Environmental Policy Act, and the Clean Water Act.

[32] 73 Fed. Reg. 76272 (December 16, 2008) (effective January 15, 2009).

[33] 74 Fed. Reg. 20421 (May 8, 2009) ("With this final rule, the Department of the Interior and the Department of Commerce amend regulations governing interagency cooperation under [the ESA]. In accordance with the statutory authority set forth in the 2009 Omnibus Appropriations Act (P.L. 111-8), this rule implements the regulations that were in effect immediately before the effective date of the regulation issued on December 16, 2008").

[34] 73 Fed. Reg. at 47872.

[35] 50 C.F.R. §402.02.

[36] 50 C.F.R. §17.40(q)(4). The polar bear was listed under the act primarily due to shrinking habitat caused by changing climate. 73 Fed. Reg. 28,212 (2008). The polar bear regulation prevents a lawsuit claiming that a power plant in any state other than Alaska harmed the polar bear by indirectly causing its ice floe habitat to diminish. The law that authorized revocation of the regulations discussed above, P.L. 111-8, also authorized revocation of the polar bear rule, but the Secretary of the Interior and the Secretary of Commerce did not act on that authority to revoke the rule.

[37] U.S. Const. amend. V: "[N]or shall private property be taken for public use, without just compensation."

sink, in the form of dissolved carbon dioxide, forests and wetlands are significant repositories. The "public interest review" conducted by the Corps of Engineers when applications are submitted for wetlands development[38] would seem sufficiently broad to allow Corps consideration of a wetland's carbon-sink value. Again, however, research fails to reveal any court decisions as yet. Historically, though, takings challenges to development prohibitions in wetlands have shown a better chance of success than with development prohibitions generally, because a development-barred wetland may have no economic use whatsoever.

E. Consideration of Climate Change in Environmental Impact Statements

It is no longer in doubt that the National Environmental Policy Act (NEPA)[39] requires a federal agency to consider climate change impacts—those the agency's proposed project may contribute to, and those affecting the proposed project—in environmental impact statements (EISs).[40] The very first appearance of climate change in a reported court decision was in a NEPA case,[41] and the numerous NEPA/climate-change decisions since have never doubted that where sufficiently serious and causally connected to the project, climate change impacts should be discussed.[42] Draft guidance from the Council on Environmental Quality (CEQ) also makes the point.[43]

Still, clear thresholds triggering EIS inclusion have yet to emerge from the court decisions. CEQ suggests in its draft guidance that when federal activity is subject to GHG emissions accounting requirements, such as CAA reporting requirements that apply to stationary sources that directly emit 25,000 metric tons or more of CO_2-equivalent GHG on an annual basis, the agency should include this information in the NEPA documentation for consideration by decision makers and the public. CEQ expressly disclaims, however, that it intends 25,000 metric tons per year as the emission level that constitutes a "major federal action significantly affecting the quality of the human environment,"[44] NEPA's trigger for requiring an agency to prepare an EIS.

In addition to the federal NEPA, many states have NEPA-like statutes for evaluating proposals of state agencies. A full review of the legal issues raised by climate change under these "little

---

[38] 33 C.F.R. §320.4 ("The decision whether to issue a permit will be based on an evaluation of the probable impacts, including cumulative impacts, of the proposed activity and its intended use on the public interest.").

[39] 42 U.S.C. §§4321-4370f.

[40] *See* NEPA §102(2)(C); 42 U.S.C. §4332(2)(C).

[41] City of Los Angeles v. National Highway Traffic Safety Admin., 912 F.2d 478 (D.C. Cir. 1990).

[42] *See, e.g.,* Center for Biological Diversity v. National Highway Traffic Safety Admin., 508 F.3d 508, 550 (9th Cir. 2007) ("The impact of greenhouse gas emissions is precisely the kind of cumulative impacts analysis that NEPA requires agencies to conduct.").

[43] CEQ, Memorandum for Heads of Federal Departments and Agencies, *Draft NEPA Guidance on Consideration of the Effects of Climate Change and Greenhouse Gas Emissions* (February 18, 2010). As to a proposed project's possible contribution to climate change, the guidance states that "where a proposed Federal action that is analyzed in an [environmental assessment] or EIS would be anticipated to emit GHGs to the atmosphere in quantities that the agency finds may be meaningful, it is appropriate for the agency to quantify and disclose its estimate of the expected annual direct and indirect GHG emissions in the environmental documentation for the proposed action." *Id.* at 2. As to a proposed project's potential for being affected by future climate change, the guidance is equally unequivocal: "CEQ proposes that agencies should determine which climate change impacts warrant consideration in their [environmental assessments] and EISs because of their impact on the analysis of the environmental effects of a proposed agency action." *Id.* at 6.

[44] NEPA §102(2)(C); 42 U.S.C. §4332(2)(C).

NEPAs" is beyond the scope of this report. An example is the split in the California courts on whether projected future conditions (as in a climate-changed world) rather than current ones can be used as the baseline for evaluating the environmental impacts of proposed state projects.[45]

F. Carbon capture and sequestration[46]

While most proposals to mitigate climate change have focused on limiting GHG emissions, a prominent mitigation alternative is carbon capture and sequestration (CCS). CCS is a process whereby CO_2 emissions would be "captured" at their source and then stored or "sequestered" either underground or elsewhere, rather than being released into the atmosphere. Frequently, this storage/sequestration would take place underground.

Large-scale CCS technology is still in the early stages of development. Therefore, there are a number of operational questions to be answered before we can fully understand all the legal issues that may arise. However, because the development of CCS technology could well depend in part upon the resolution of some of these legal issues, it is important to understand them as the CCS debate continues. Among the emerging legal issues associated with CCS technology are (1) who owns and controls the underground pore space where the CO_2 would be "sequestered" under many of the CCS facility concepts proposed, in particular is pore space part of the surface estate or mineral rights under traditional property law principles; (2) which federal and state agencies would permit and regulate CO_2 pipelines transporting the gas from the point of generation to the sequestration site under the existing framework for pipeline regulation; and (3) concerns over liability exposure that may hinder development of CCS technology.[47]

G. Constitutional barriers to state action

Two federal constitutional constraints on state action, preemption and the dormant commerce clause, have played a role in blocking state efforts to restrict GHG emissions.

1. Preemption

Two federal statutes have been invoked to argue for federal preemption of state laws affecting GHG emissions: the CAA and the Energy Policy and Conservation Act (EPCA). The CAA, while not generally preempting state regulation of stationary source emissions, does preempt state standards "relating to" the control of emissions from new motor vehicles.[48] An exception is that EPA may waive CAA preemption for vehicle emission standards in California, should that state so request,[49] whereupon states with standards identical to California's also participate in the

---

[45] Compare *Sunnyvale West Neighborhood Ass'n v. City of Sunnyvale City Council*, 190 Cal. App. 4th 1351, 1382-1383 (2010) and *Madera Oversight Coalition, Inc. v. City of Madera*, 199 Cal. App. 4th 48, 90 (2011), each finding use of future conditions as the baseline to be improper, with *Neighbors for Smart Rail v. Exposition Metro Line Construction Authority*, No. B232655 (Cal. App. filed April 17, 2012), holding that in a proper case, use of projected conditions may be appropriate way to measure impacts project will have on traffic, air quality, and GHG emissions.

[46] This section of the report was written by Adam Vann, Legislative Attorney, CRS American Law Division.

[47] For a detailed discussion of these issues, see CRS Report RL34307, *Legal Issues Associated with the Development of Carbon Dioxide Sequestration Technology*, by Adam Vann and Paul W. Parfomak.

[48] CAA §209(a); 42 U.S.C. §7543(a).

[49] CAA §209(b); 42 U.S.C. §7543(b).

waiver.[50] EPCA, for its part, is not directly concerned with emissions. Rather, it authorizes federal promulgation of corporate average fuel economy standards ("CAFE standards"),[51] then dictates that when a CAFE standard is in effect, a state may not regulate in a manner "related to" such fuel economy standards.[52] No California waiver or other waiver is authorized.

An obvious ambiguity exists as to when a state action is "relating to" or "related to" the relevant federal action, and thus preempted. For example, one case dealt with city regulations reducing the rates at which taxicab owners could lease vehicles to drivers if the vehicle did not have a hybrid engine. The court found it "likely" (the standard for obtaining a preliminary injunction) that the regulations effectively required cab owners to buy only hybrid vehicles, so that the regulations were "relating to" the control of emissions under the CAA and "related to" CAFE standards under EPCA. So finding, the court held that plaintiffs had shown a likelihood of success in showing preemption, and a preliminary injunction was granted.[53]

It is also unclear at what point a state's actions restricting GHG emissions are preempted as interfering with national foreign policy, given the long history of U.S. involvement in international negotiations over GHG emissions.[54] The issue has been raised in litigation.[55]

2. Dormant Commerce Clause

Quite recently, in *Rocky Mountain Farmers Union v. Goldstene*, a federal district court ruled that California's Low Carbon Fuel Standard (LCFS) offends the Constitution's "dormant commerce clause."[56] The dormant commerce clause, a judicially created corollary of the Constitution's Commerce Clause,[57] bars a state from discriminating against commerce based on its out-of-state origin, and, even in the absence of discrimination, bars a state from imposing "undue burdens" on interstate commerce. Here, the court found that the LCFS discriminated against out-of-state corn-derived ethanol while favoring in-state corn ethanol, and impermissibly regulated extraterritorial conduct. In addition, said the court, the state had failed to show a lack of alternative, nondiscriminatory ways to reduce GHG emissions. The LCFS regulations are a part of California's attempts, under a state enactment, to reduce GHG emissions in California to 1990 levels by 2020.[58]

---

[50] CAA §177; 42 U.S.C. §7507.

[51] 49 U.S.C. §32902(a).

[52] 49 U.S.C. §32919.

[53] Metropolitan Taxicab Bd. of Trade v. City of New York, 633 F. Supp. 2d 83, *aff'd as to EPCA*, 615 F.3d 152 (2d Cir. 2010), *cert. denied*, 131 S. Ct. 1569 (2011).

[54] As the Supreme Court noted in *Massachusetts v. EPA*, 549 U.S. 497, 519 (2007): "Massachusetts ... cannot negotiate [a GHG] emissions treaty with China or India ...." The leading decision on foreign policy preemption is *American Insurance Ass'n v. Garamendi*, 539 U.S. 396 (2003).

[55] *See, e.g.,* Green Mountain Chrysler Plymouth Dodge v. Crombie, 508 F. Supp. 2d 295 (D. Vt. 2007) (no foreign policy preemption found of Vermont's GHG emission standards for new automobiles).

[56] 2011 Westlaw 6934797 (E.D. Cal. December 29, 2011), *appealing pending before Ninth Circuit*. By separate order, the court concluded that CAA §211(c)(4)(B) failed to give California immunity from dormant commerce clause challenge. The court declined for the moment to decide plaintiffs' preemption argument.

[57] U.S. Const. art. I, §8, cl. 3.

[58] Global Warming Solutions Act of 2006 (AB 32), Cal. Health & Safety Code §38,500 et seq. The LCFS regulation is at Cal. Code Regs. tit. 17, §§95,480-95,490.

An intriguing question is whether *Rocky Mountain Farmers Union* may lead to other climate-change-related dormant commerce clause challenges. One possible object of such challenges might be California's cap-and-trade system—in particular, its requirement that importers of electricity account for their emissions. Another might be SB 1368, a 2006 California law that set an "emission performance standard" for all long-term power contracts and baseload generation. The standard was set at 1,100 pounds of CO_2 per megawatt-hour. Since most of the generation that exceeds that standard is located outside California (in the coal states of Wyoming and Montana), the law might be seen to overburden out-of-state competitors.[59]

H. The Public Trust Doctrine and GHG Emissions

In May 2011, a coordinated campaign of lawsuits and rulemaking petitions was initiated based on the argument that (1) the states and the federal government have a public trust responsibility to protect the atmosphere, and (2) with regard to climate change, they have failed to exercise that responsibility.[60] Either a lawsuit (about 12) or a petition (about 40) was filed in each state. The lawsuits and petitions, many filed by minors through their guardians ad litem, are being coordinated by Our Children's Trust, an Oregon nonprofit.

As background, the public trust doctrine is an ancient common law principle with origins in Roman law and the Magna Carta. It asserts that certain natural resources are held by the sovereign in special status. Key aspects of that special status are that government may neither alienate public trust resources nor, more pertinent here, permit their injury by private parties. Rather, government has an affirmative duty to safeguard these resources for the benefit of the general public. The doctrine is generally a principle of state law, though there is limited recognition of a federal counterpart. After tidelands and the beds of navigable waterways, fish and wildlife are the natural resources most traditionally associated with the public trust doctrine; courts do not appear to have applied the doctrine to the atmosphere yet, as the suits and petitions here are seeking.

As for the lawsuits, each one reportedly asks the court for declaratory relief proclaiming that the atmosphere is a public trust resource and that the government in question has a fiduciary duty as trustee to protect it. Some of the suits ask for injunctive relief as well. For example, the suit against the United States asserts that the federal government has violated its trustee duties by allowing unsafe amounts of GHGs into the atmosphere and asks for an injunction requiring it to take action "consistent with the United States government's equitable share of the global effort."[61]

The trend in the early litigation results has been against the plaintiffs—state trial courts finding, for example, that the public trust doctrine does not apply to the atmosphere,[62] or that the doctrine is not recognized in the state.[63] As yet there have been no rulings that a state, pursuant to the

---

[59] *See* Debra Kahn, *Traders worry that a Calif. low-carbon fuels decision could apply to electricity imports*, E&E Climatewire (January 20, 2012).

[60] For further details, see CRS Report R41496, *Common-Law Climate Change Litigation After American Electric Power v. Connecticut*, by Robert Meltz.

[61] Alec L. v. Jackson, No. 11-cv-2203 (N.D. Cal. filed May 4, 2011) (complaint at 17). In December, 2011, the case was transferred to the U.S. District Court for the District of Columbia.

[62] *See, e.g.,* Aronow v. Minnesota Dep't of Pollution Control, No. 62-CV-11-3952 (Minn. D. Ct. January 30, 2012), *appeal pending before Minnesota Court of Appeals.*

[63] Martinez v. State of Colorado, No. 11CV4377 (Colo. D. Ct. November 7, 2011).

---

public trust doctrine, must act to address climate change. The suit against the United States was dismissed by the district court on the grounds that (1) the public trust doctrine is a purely state law doctrine, so a federal court lacks jurisdiction, and (2) under *American Electric Power v. Connecticut*,[64] use of the public trust doctrine in the air pollution context has been displaced by the Clean Air Act.[65] On the other hand, preliminary rulings favorable to plaintiffs have come from Texas and New Mexico. In Texas, the district court ruled that, owing to its presence in the state constitution, the public trust doctrine "includes all natural resources of the State," including the atmosphere, but that owing to pending litigation on whether the Texas Clean Air Act covers GHGs, the state's refusal to exercise its GHG authority was reasonable.[66] In New Mexico, the district court found that plaintiff's claim was not appropriate for disposition at the pleading stage.[67] As for the rulemaking petitions, these have been denied in at least 27 jurisdictions.[68]

The generally negative results of the public trust litigation and petitions thus far are not surprising. As much as because the suits and petitions seek a major expansion of the public trust doctrine, courts are traditionally reluctant to obtrude into matters, such as global climate change, that go beyond the capabilities of a court to manage.

III. Liability for Harms Caused by Climate Change

Based on consensus predictions as to the many harms that climate change may cause, one may safely predict that liability lawsuits will be filed. This report previously mentioned the standing hurdle looming before climate change plaintiffs, especially those that are not states, and the political question hurdle. Following are some additional issues in liability actions.

A. Liability After *American Electric Power Co., Inc. v. Connecticut*

In *American Electric Power Co., Inc. v. Connecticut*,[69] the Supreme Court read the CAA to bar federal judges from imposing their own limits on GHG emissions from fossil-fuel-fired power plants, separate from those imposed by EPA under that act. More formally, the Court held that the CAA displaces any federal common law of nuisance that might ground a claim seeking judicial abatement of such emissions. However, *American Electric Power* left open two key questions. First, may those suffering climate-change impacts still assert federal common law of nuisance actions seeking not injunctive relief, as plaintiffs sought in *American Electric Power*, but rather *monetary damages*? Second, do *state law* claims, either common law or statutory, withstand *American Electric Power*, which addressed only *federal* common law claims?

Recently, both these questions were answered in the negative. In *Comer v. Murphy Oil Co.*, Mississippi land owners pressed state and federal tort claims (nuisance, trespass, and negligence)

---

[64] 131 S. Ct. 2527 (2011). *See* Section III.A. of this report.

[65] Alec L. v. Jackson, No. 11-cv-02235 (D.D.C. May 31, 2012).

[66] Angela Bonser-Lain v. Texas Comm'n on Envtl. Quality, No. D-1-GN-11-002194 (Tex. D. Ct. July 9, 2012) (letter ruling).

[67] Akilah Sanders-Reed v. Martinez, No. D-101-CV-2011-01514 (N.M. D. Ct. July 14, 2012).

[68] *See* http://climatelawyers.com/post/2012/02/04/Aronow-v-Minnesota-is-Dismissed-Public-Trust-Doctrine-Not-Extended-to-the-Atmosphere-in-Minnesota.aspx.

[69] 131 S. Ct. 2527 (2011).

against numerous oil, coal, and chemical companies that allegedly emitted substantial GHGs.[70] The land owners' claims were based on property-related harms suffered as the result of Hurricane Katrina—they argued that the defendants, through their GHG emissions and resulting climate change, had contributed to warmer ocean temperatures that had intensified the hurricane, and to rising sea level that aggravated the hurricane's impacts further. They sought damages. Despite the differences from *American Electric Power*—state rather than federal claims, monetary rather than injunctive relief—the district court had little difficulty finding that decision controlling. Here as in *American Electric Power*, the court said, the lawsuit called upon the court to determine what level of CO_2 emissions was unreasonable, a determination the Supreme Court explained had been entrusted by Congress to the EPA. Therefore, the court determined that the plaintiffs' "entire lawsuit" is displaced by the CAA,[71] though the ruling is dictum.[72]

The reach of *American Electric Power* may soon be tackled again in the appeal of the district court decision in *Native Village of Kivalina v. ExxonMobil Corp.*[73] In this case, Inupiat Eskimos forced to relocate their coastal village due to shore erosion sued 20 energy and utility companies for damages. Their claim was that the defendants' GHG emissions had, by exacerbating climate change, contributed to the melting of sea ice that had protected the village's shores from wave erosion. The district court decision, rendered prior to *American Electric Power*, rejected the claim on standing and political question grounds. These issues will be before the circuit court, of course, in addition to the displacement question under *American Electric Power*.

B. Insurance Coverage of Injury or Liability Associated With Climate Change

Federal and private insurers are well aware that if the scientific consensus is correct that climate change will bring on more frequent extreme weather events, they stand to make substantially increased payments.[74] At this time, there appear to be no insurance policies that provide explicit coverage for injuries resulting from climate change; however, there are policies that cover many of the injuries likely to be associated with climate change, "such as flood, wind, freezing, heat, earth movement, or collapse."[75]

---

[70] 839 F. Supp. 2d 849 (S.D. Miss. 2012).

[71] *Id.* at *14.

[72] When a court rules on an issue not required for resolution of the case, the ruling is referred to as "dictum." Traditionally, dictum is entitled to less precedential force than a pronouncement of the court essential to disposing of the case—often termed a "holding." In *Comer*, the *American Electric Power* discussion described in text above was preceded by not one, but three, different determinations of the court (res judicata, absence of standing, and nonjusticiale political question) each one of which was fully adequate to support dismissal of the action. That is, the court had no need to resolve the displacement issue and its discussion is, therefore, dictum.

[73] 663 F. Supp. 2d 863 (N.D. Cal. 2009), *appeal pending before Ninth Circuit*.

[74] Evan Lehmann, *Reinsurers press Congress to reduce U.S. risk from climate change (E&E ClimateWire* March 2, 2012); Evan Lehmann, *Disasters, continuing to climb, inflict record insurance losses in 2011* (E&E ClimateWire January 5, 2012); Government Accountability Office, *Climate Change Financial Risks to Federal and Private Insurers in Coming Decades Are Potentially Significant*, GAO-07-760T (2007). For general background, see Gary S. Guzy, "Insurance and Climate Change," in Michael B. Gerrard (ed.), GLOBAL CLIMATE CHANGE AND U.S. LAW (ABA 2007); Justin Pidot, Georgetown Envtl. Law and Policy Inst., *Coastal Disaster Insurance in the Era of Global Warming* (2007) (copy on file with author); Adam Riedel, *California, New York and Washington to Require Insurers to Provide Information on Climate Change Risks*, available at blogs.law.columbia.edu/climate change/2012/02/06.

[75] *Guzy, supra* note 74, at 554.

Some issues in the vast universe of insurance-coverage litigation seem to be especially relevant to climate change. One arises from coastal hurricanes, the impacts of which may be exacerbated by climate-change-induced sea level rise. The issue is whether a particular item of hurricane damage is to be regarded as wind-caused damage or flood-caused damage. The distinction is pivotal because domestic insurance policies cover only wind damage; flood damage is insured under the National Flood Insurance Program.[76] The litigation in this area, such as that generated by Hurricane Katrina, is voluminous and often turns on factual questions, but also raises such issues as (1) who, insurer or insured, bears the burden of showing the portion of damage covered by the policy when both an insured (say, wind-caused) risk and a non-insured (say, flooding-caused) risk contributed;[77] (2) whether water driven by wind ("storm surge") falls outside the flooding exclusion in homeowners' policies;[78] and (3) whether the flooding exclusion covers man-made causes (e.g., negligent maintenance of levees) as well as natural ones.[79]

Another issue is whether the Comprehensive General Liability (CGL) policy used by businesses covers liability imposed on the insured as the result of the insured's GHG emissions, when those emissions contribute to climate-change-related damage. The only known decision on this issue is *AES Corp. v. Steadfast Ins. Co.*,[80] a ruling by the Virginia Supreme Court that the insurance company was not obligated to provide defense under its CGL policy with AES in the *Kivalina* suit,[81] because Kivalina's complaint did not allege an "occurrence."

Finally, some policies, such as environmental liability or pollution policies, cover damage from "pollution." Where "pollution" is defined in policies to mean substances classified as pollutants under environmental laws, the Supreme Court decision in *Massachusetts v. EPA* may prove pivotal.[82] There, the Court held that GHG emissions are "air pollutants" under the Clean Air Act, raising the possibility that this ruling will be used to enlarge policy coverage to bring in damage traceable to GHG emissions.

C. U.S. Liability in International Fora Based on GHG Emissions

Whether sovereign nations may be, or should be, liable under international law for failing to reduce GHG emissions within their territory has long attracted the attention of commentators[83]— and, of course, low-lying nations. However, research fails to reveal any successful effort to impose such liability.

Some principles that might be applied to a claim alleging GHG-caused injury might be taken from the international law of transboundary pollution. For example, the Restatement (Third) of Foreign Relations Law describes an international law principle under which a nation must "take

---

[76] 42 U.S.C. §§4001-4029.

[77] *See, e.g.*, Bayle v. Allstate Ins. Co., 615 F.3d 350 (5th Cir. 2010).

[78] *See, e.g.*, Leonard v. Nationwide Ins. Co., 499 F.3d 419 (5th Cir. 2007).

[79] *See, e.g.*, In re Katrina Canal Breaches Litigation, 495 F.3d 191 (5th Cir. 2007).

[80] 715 S.E.2d 28 (Va. 2011), *motion for rehearing granted Jan. 17, 2012.*

[81] See description of this decision in text accompanying note 73 *supra*.

[82] 549 U.S. 497 (2011).

[83] *See* Michael Faure et al., CLIMATE CHANGE LIABILITY (2011); Richard Lord et al. (eds.), CLIMATE CHANGE LIABILITY: TRANSNATIONAL LAW AND PRACTICE (2012); Timo Koivurova, *International Legal Avenues to Address the Plight of Victims of Climate Change*, 62 J. Envtl. L. & Litig. 269 (2007); Andrew L. Strauss, *The Legal Option Suing the United States in International Forums for Global Warming Emissions*, 33 Envtl. L. Rptr. 10185 (2003).

---

such measures as may be necessary, to the extent practicable under the circumstances, to ensure that activities within its jurisdiction or control ... are conducted so as not to cause significant injury to the environment of another state."[84] Similarly, the *Trail Smelter* arbitration decision, probably the seminal ruling on state liability for transboundary pollution, declared that "[a] State owes at all times a duty to protect other States against injurious acts by individuals from within its jurisdiction."[85] Of course, as with the domestic litigation, daunting hurdles confront the international-law claimant in making the link between climate change in general and specific environmental harms, and in apportioning how much of such harms to attribute to the charged parties.

Research reveals only one climate-change-related international law action filed against the United States. In 2005, the chair of the Inuit Circumpolar Conference, on behalf of herself and all affected Inuit of the arctic regions of the United States and Canada, filed a petition against the United States with the Inter-American Commission on Human Rights, the investigative arm of the Organization of American States (OAS).[86] The petition alleged that the United States, through its failure to restrict its GHG emissions and the resultant climate change, had violated the Inuit's human rights—including their rights to their culture, to property, to the preservation of health, life, and to physical integrity. Inuit culture is described in the petition as "inseparable from the condition of [its] physical surroundings."[87] Generally, the Inter-American Commission on Human Rights is empowered to recommend measures that contribute to human rights protection, request states in urgent cases to adopt specific precautionary measures to avoid serious harm to human rights, or submit cases to the Inter-American Court of Human Rights. The United States, however, has not accepted the jurisdiction of this court, so the Inuit petition sought only to have the commission prepare a report declaring the responsibilities of the United States and recommending corrective measures.

In 2006, the Commission informed the petitioner that it would not process the petition "at present," explaining that "the information provided does not enable us to determine whether the alleged facts would tend to characterize a violation of rights protected by the American Declaration."[88]

---

[84] RESTATEMENT (THIRD) OF FOREIGN RELATIONS LAW §601(1). *See also* Legality of the Threat or Use of Nuclear Weapons, Advisory Opinion, 1996 ICJ Reports 226, 241-242 (July 8, 1996) ("the existence of the general obligation of states to ensure that activities within their jurisdiction and control respect the environment of other states or of areas beyond national control is now part of the corpus of international law relating to the environment").

[85] Trail Smelter (U.S. v. Canada), 3 R.I.A.A. 1938, 1965 (March 11, 1941).

[86] Petition to the Inter American Commission on Human Rights Seeking Relief from Violations Resulting from Global Warming Caused by Actions and Omissions of the United States, *available at* http://inuitcircumpolar.com/files/uploads/icc-files/FINALPetitionICC.pdf. For detailed discussion of the petition, see Koivurova, *supra* note 83, at 285.

[87] *Id.* at 5.

[88] Letter from Ariel E. Dulitzky, Ass't Executive Sec'y, Inter-American Commission on Human Rights, to Sheila Watt-Cloutier (November 16, 2006), *available at* http://graphics8.nytimes.com/packages/pdf/science/16commissionletter.pdf. The "American Declaration" referred to by the Commission is the American Declaration of the Rights and Duties of Man, OAS Res. XXX, *available at* http://www1.umn.edu/humanrts/oasinstr/zoas2dec.htm.

IV. Climate Change-Induced Water Shortages

A. Water Scarcity and Water Rights

It is widely predicted that climate change will exacerbate water scarcity—widening arid areas and making them even drier. The future of the western United States has received substantial attention in this regard.[89] Where demand outstrips supply, the nature and flexibility of existing water rights are raised.

To be sure, water rights, mostly a creature of state law, are property of a uniquely conditional nature. Most obviously, the water rights holder does not own the water to which the right applies; the right is merely "usufructuary," that is, to *use* the water. In the western United States, water rights generally are governed by "prior appropriation" doctrine, under which the right of use is contingent on the right holder putting the water to "beneficial use," and is further subject to common law or statutory limits based on the public trust doctrine and the doctrine of reasonable use. With regard to "reasonable use," the California Constitution, as an example, declares that the "unreasonable use or unreasonable method of use of water be prevented," a doctrine that is self-executing and evolving.[90] Appropriation doctrine is a "first in time, first in right" system under which inadequate supply results in junior-in-time appropriators having their water cut before senior-in-time appropriators.

Despite the conditionality of water rights, it remains to be seen how much latitude government agencies have to respond to periods of water scarcity by cutting back on the consumption of vested water rights holders to accommodate critical public needs. It is also unclear to what extent appropriation doctrine states may allow water rights holders to transfer water rights, generally favored by scholars as promoting more efficient outcomes and the achieving of environmental goals.[91] One writer has noted that in the West, the explosive population growth of recent decades has often occurred in communities with only junior water rights. Senior water rights holders often include older municipalities, mining, and agriculture.[92] The question then arises whether reasonable use and other doctrines qualifying appropriation water rights can address the difficult situation of new communities being starved for water while senior appropriators endure little or no reduction in water supplies.

States have evolved a variety of additional mechanisms for allocating water among rights holders in times of scarcity. Many states exempt certain "domestic" uses of water (e.g., for stock watering, home use, or lawn watering) from the general permit scheme. If climate change produces more droughts, conflicts will increase between exempted users and those with appropriation rights, especially senior appropriators. In some cases, the ability of an exempted

---

[89] See the discussion of the possible effects of climate change on water availability in the western United States in Priyanka Sundareshan, *Using the Transfer of Water Rights as a Climate Change Adaptation Strategy Comparing the United States and Australia*, 27 Ariz. J. Int'l & Comp. L. 911, 920-921 (2010).

[90] Cal Const. art. 10, §2 (describing the principles of beneficial use and reasonableness as "self-executing"); State Water Resources Control Bd. v. Forni, 126 Cal. Rptr. 851 (1976) (noting that "[w]hat is a [reasonable and] beneficial use at one time may, because of changed conditions, become a waste of water at a later time").

[91] Sundareshan, *supra* note 89, at 923-925.

[92] Joel Smith et al., Georgetown Climate Center, *Adaptation Case Studies in the Western United States* at 22 (2011) (writing with specific reference to Colorado's prior appropriation doctrine).

---

user to leapfrog over the rights of senior appropriators may be held subject to payment of compensation under the constitutional right to compensation for the taking of property.[93]

The issues raised above are also likely to arise in the context of groundwater, which, as with surface water, is usually held under a right of use only, not outright ownership.[94] A recent Texas Supreme Court decision adopted the minority view of outright ownership, the court reassuring that conservation of groundwater still can be done without takings as long as the problems of limited water supply "are shared by the public, not foisted onto a few."[95]

B. Water Diversion and Delivery Cutbacks

Periods of low precipitation, as may be more frequent in the future due to climate change, have generated several court decisions where the conflict was between the water needs of the public and those of fish in streams. These decisions resolved claims of Fifth Amendment takings of water rights and claims of government breach of water-supply contracts based on cutbacks in the amount of water delivered from federal water projects—as demanded by the Endangered Species Act[96] and the Central Valley Improvement Act.[97] A key issue in these cases has been whether the taking claim is to be analyzed by the court as a physical taking of the water, or as a regulatory taking of use rights in the water. The distinction matters a great deal. In general, a plaintiff's litigation prospects are substantially improved if the court adopts a physical takings framework, thus the physical versus regulatory takings issue has been hard fought in the courts. Currently, it appears that when the government requires a *physical diversion of the water* away from the plaintiff's desired use (as to operate a fish ladder), the plaintiff-friendly physical taking approach is triggered.[98] But, it would appear, not otherwise.

Another issue has been the role of doctrines that qualify water rights—principally, public trust and reasonable use.[99] Do these doctrines allow the government to set supervening public priorities for fish preservation as part of rights it retains when conferring water rights? If the government

---

[93] *See, e.g.*, Bassinger v. Taylor, 164 P. 522, 523 (Idaho 1917).

[94] Again using California as our example, that state's Supreme Court has explained that "overlying water rights are usufructuary only, and while conferring the legal right to use the water that is superior to all other users, confer no private right of ownership in public waters." City of Barstow v. Mohave Water Agency, 5 P.3d 853, 860 n.7 (2000). An illustrative decision on a takings challenge to a county restriction on withdrawal of groundwater (not, so far as appears, for climate change reasons) is Allegretti & Co. v. County of Imperial, 42 Cal. Rptr. 3d 122 (Cal. App. 2006) (no physical or regulatory taking caused by 12,000 acre-feet per year limit imposed by county in groundwater withdrawal permit).

[95] Edwards Aquifer Auth. v. Day, 2012 WL 592729 *20 (Tex. February 24, 2012).

[96] Tulare Lake Basin Water Storage Dist. v. United States, 49 Fed. Cl. 313 (2001); Klamath Irrigation Dist. v. United States, 635 F.3d 505 (Fed. Cir. 2011); Casitas Municipal Water Dist. v. United States, 2011 Westlaw 6017935 (Fed. Cl. December 5, 2011).

[97] Stockton East Water Dist. v. United States, 101 Fed. Cl. 352 (2011).

[98] Casitas Municipal Water Dist. v. United States, 543 F.3d 1276 (Fed. Cir. 2008). On remand, the trial court found the claim unripe, 102 Fed. Cl. 443 (Fed. Cl. 2011), a determination now on appeal back to the Federal Circuit.

[99] As explained in the *Casitas* remand, 102 Fed. Cl. at 455, with reference to the state of California:

> Under the public trust doctrine, state agencies have the responsibility to protect trust resources associated with California's waterways, such as navigation, fisheries, recreation, ecological preservation, and related beneficial uses. .... Similarly, the reasonable use doctrine prohibits the waste, unreasonable use, unreasonable method of use, and unreasonable method of diversion of water. (citations omitted)

---

retains such rights, no taking claim can succeed, for the water rights holder cannot be found to have suffered a taking of a right he or she never acquired.

V. Sea Level Rise and Extreme Precipitation

A. Effect of Sea Level Rise on the Beachfront Owner's Property Line

Sea level rise generally causes the boundary between land and water to move landward.[100] The common law has long had to deal with such shifting boundaries—in particular, with who owns land newly dry or newly submerged. The rule, dating back to Roman times, turns on whether the land-water boundary shift occurred slowly or quickly.[101] When land-water boundaries shift *gradually and imperceptibly*—"so slowly that one could not see the change occurring"[102]—the ownership boundary shifts with it. Thus, in the case of "accretion," defined as the gradual depositing of alluvion (sand, sediment, or other deposits) so as to enlarge one's tract, the owner of the tract becomes the happy owner of the accreted area as well. The shore owner may be less pleased, however, with "erosion," the gradual and imperceptible boundary shift towards land when former upland is submerged. As with accretion, the property line moves—landward this time.[103]

In contrast with accretion and erosion, *sudden* shifts in the land-water boundary, known regardless of direction as "avulsion," do not shift ownership lines. A classic avulsive event is a hurricane that abruptly shifts the mean high water mark on a beach either seaward or landward. In this case, the property line between the owner of the intertidal zone and permanently submerged lands (typically the state in trust for the public) and the owner of uplands beyond the high water mark (typically a private entity) does not move.

The pivotal question is whether movement in the land-water boundary owing to climate-change-caused sea level rise is fast enough to be avulsive, leaving the property line unmoved, or gradual enough to be erosion, reducing the shoreowner's property.[104] No caselaw on the point exists and commentators are divided. One scholar asserts: "The rising sea level [from climate change] is neither gradual like traditional accretion, erosion, or reliction; nor is it sudden and violent like traditional avulsion. We are facing a historically distinct situation that is not a good factual fit with the [traditional common law] rules."[105] Two other scholars, in contrast, do see the requisite

---

[100] In some locations, sea level relative to the adjacent land has "fallen" because the land has risen more than the sea level. Land may rise once relieved of the massive weight of retreating glaciers as the result of climate change, natural and human-induced. Cornelia Dean, *As Alaska Glaciers Melt, It's Land That's Rising*, New York Times, May 19, 2009, at A1.

[101] *See generally* James G. Titus, *Rising Seas, Coastal Erosion, and the Takings Clause How to Save Wetlands and Beaches Without Hurting Property Owners*, 57 Md. L. Rev. 1279 (1998).

[102] Stop the Beach Renourishment, Inc. v.. Florida Dep't of Envtl. Prot., 130 S. Ct. 2592, 2598 (2010).

[103] *See, e.g.,* City of Long Branch v. Jui Yung Liu, 4 A.3d 542, 550 (N.J. 2010).

[104] Identifying the portion of coastal erosion attributable to sea level rise may be a challenge. One writer notes: "In many Gulf of Mexico states, ... the projected rate of beach loss due to sea level rise is overwhelmed by the current background rate of erosion." Donna M. Christie, *Sea Level Rise and Gulf Beaches The Specter of Judicial Takings*, 26 J. Land Use & Envtl. L. 313, 314 (2011).

[105] *See* Joe Sax, *Some Unorthodox Thoughts About Rising Sea Levels, Beach Erosion and Property Rights*, 11 Vt. J. (continued...)

---

gradualness for property line movement: "in most instances sea level rise [from climate change] will transform private property into public property as sea waters cover formerly dry land."[106]

Case law authority does suggest that public trust ownership of coastal submerged lands and the adjacent intertidal zone (between low and high water mark) expands automatically when erosion occurs. That is, no legal process is required. In *McQueen v. South Carolina Coastal Council*, for example, that state's high court decreed that under state law, wetlands created by the encroachment of navigable tidal water belong to the state—that is, are public trust property. Proof that such lands were upland when acquired and that the tidelands were subsequently created by the rising of tidal water, said the court, cannot defeat the state's presumptive title to the tidelands.[107] As well, the court held, the state incurs no takings liability.

As long as state courts are able to ground such extensions of public trust lands in traditional common law, no Fifth Amendment taking from beachfront property owners is likely to be discerned. Title to coastal property (or any other property) is assumed to be qualified by traditional common law principles, and public trust doctrine certainly falls in this category. On the other hand, if courts use sea level rise as an occasion to expand public trust doctrine beyond its traditional state-law parameters or to otherwise shrink littoral rights, the possibility of a so-called "judicial taking" may arise. This novel concept, that *courts* may effect takings just as other branches of government do, received a major boost in 2010 when a Supreme Court plurality proposed that "[i]f a legislature *or a court* declares that what was once an established right of private property no longer exists, it has taken that property."[108] As yet, however, no court has ever found a judicial taking in a final decision.

B. "Rolling" Public Beach Access Easements

A case out of Texas is being closely watched as suggestive of constitutional issues that may be raised by landward migration of beaches from climate-change-related sea level rise. Though the case involves landward migration as the result of a hurricane, it could just as easily have arisen in connection with sea level rise (or hurricane impacts enhanced by sea level rise).

Severance v. Patterson[109] deals with the Texas Open Beaches Act, which imposes a public access easement on the state's beaches extending landward to the dune vegetation line. The lower Texas courts had long construed this access easement to "roll"—that is, to migrate with movements in the dune vegetation line. The consequence is that landward movement of the vegetation line may

---

(...continued)

Envtl. L. 641, 645 (2010).

[106] J. Peter Byrne and Jessica Grannis, *Coastal Retreat Measures*, in Michael B. Gerrard and Katrina F. Kuh, (eds.), ADAPTATION TO CLIMATE CHANGE AND THE LAW: U.S. AND INTERNATIONAL ASPECTS (ABA, forthcoming 2012).

[107] 580 S.E.2d 116 (S.C. 2003). *See also City of Long Branch*, 4 A.3d at 550 ("[u]nder the common law, the owner of oceanfront property takes title to dry land added by accretion, but loses to the State title over land that becomes tidally flowed as a result of erosion"); Bollay v. California Office of Administrative Law, 122 Cal. Rptr. 3d 490, 493 (Cal. App. 2011) ("the mean high tide line may change over time, affecting the seaward boundary of property along the coast").

[108] Stop the Beach Renourishment, Inc. v. Florida Dep't of Envtl. Prot., 130 S. Ct. 2592, 2602 (2010) (emphasis in original). *See generally* Christie, *supra* note 104. As noted by Justice Kennedy in his *Stop the Beach* concurring opinion, the Due Process Clause also constrains state courts from substantially reducing property rights by arbitrary or irrational decision. 130 S. Ct. at 2614-2617.

[109] 566 F.3d 490 (5th Cir. 2009).

---

result in private land, including improved parcels, being newly encumbered by the easement. Under the act, the state may then order the house removed, although some compensation is provided for removal expenses. Carol Severance bought two houses behind the vegetation line, only to have Hurricane Ike a few months later move the line landward of her houses—making them subject to removal orders. She asserted Fifth Amendment takings and Fourth Amendment unreasonable seizure claims.

The Fifth Circuit found the taking claim unripe, but certified questions to the Texas Supreme Court as to Severance's Fourth Amendment claim. In its answers, the Texas Supreme Court narrowed the circumstances when the public access easement rolls.[110] It concluded that "[a]lthough existing public easements in the dry beach of Galveston's West Beach are dynamic, as natural forces cause the vegetation and the mean high tide lines to move gradually and imperceptibly, these easements do not spring or roll landward … as a result of avulsive events." In so ruling, the court reversed the decades-old interpretation of the Texas Open Beaches Act in the lower state courts, which had allowed the public access easement to roll no matter how abrupt the movement in the vegetation line. Also important, the Texas court ruling raises again the question asked in Section IV.A. as to whether climate-change-caused sea level rise should be considered gradual or avulsive.[111]

Another often-cited example of statutes anticipating landward migration of beaches are the coastal sand dune rules promulgated by a Maine state agency under that state's Natural Resources Protection Act.[112] The rules bar a project in a coastal sand dune system "if, within 100 years, the project may … be eroded as a result of changes in the shoreline such that the project is likely to be severely damaged after allowing for a two foot rise in sea level over 100 years."[113]

C. Shifting Floodplain Designations

Sea level rise and extreme rains born of climate change may cause lands not formerly subject to flooding to become so. Land use planners have long encountered resistance updating floodplain designations because such a designation alerts potential buyers that a parcel is vulnerable, possibly reducing the parcel's market value. It is unlikely, however, that a floodplain designation could, in itself, result in enough value loss to constitute a Fifth Amendment regulatory taking of a property.[114]

D. Levee-Related Issues

Damage from climate-change-caused extreme weather or sea level rise may require courts in the future to clarify federal liabilities in connection with Army Corps of Engineers levee construction and operation. The extensive litigation following the breaching and overtopping of the levees

---

[110] 2012 Westlaw 1059341 (Tex. March 30, 2012).

[111] The Fifth Circuit recently remanded *Severance* to the district court for further proceedings on the Fourth Amendment unreasonable seizure claim consistent with the Texas Supreme Court's answers to the certified questions. 2012 Westlaw 1825179 (5th Cir. May 21, 2012).

[112] 38 Me. Rev. Stat. Ann. §§480-A through 480-HH.

[113] Dep't of Envtl. Prot. Admin. Code ch. 355, §5.C.

[114] *See, e.g.*, Strother v. City of Rockwall, 358 S.W.2d 462 (Tex. App. 2012) (taking claim based on redesignation of land as floodplain defeated by, among other reasons, fact that land continued to be used for rental).

protecting New Orleans during Hurricane Katrina may be a harbinger of climate-change-related litigation in the future. CRS Report RL34131, *Flood Damage Related to Army Corps of Engineers Projects: Selected Legal Issues*, examines the potential liability of the United States in connection with Hurricane Katrina and other flooding—discussing the Federal Tort Claims Act, the Flood Control Act of 1928, and negligence theory.[115]

A quite recent decision holds that the Corps of Engineers' negligent maintenance of a shipping channel between New Orleans and the Gulf of Mexico had the effect of channeling Hurricane Katrina storm surge to the city, breaching levees. Accordingly, the court imposed tort liability on the United States.[116] Contrariwise, a takings claim based on Katrina-related damage to New Orleans, alleging the Corps' failure to adequately design, build, or maintain adequately the levees themselves, was rejected.[117] The gist of these and other decisions is that while the government has no duty to protect the public and its property from flooding, liability may be imposed where government structures worsen floods.[118]

Separate issues have been raised by the Corps' *intentional* releases of floodwaters from the Mississippi River in May 2011, following unusually heavy rainfalls combined with raised water levels due to snowmelt. These issues, mostly concerning the Corps' authority to release waters intentionally and the adequacy of the flowage easements obtained by the Corps, are also treated in CRS Report RL34131, *Flood Damage Related to Army Corps of Engineers Projects: Selected Legal Issues*, by Cynthia Brougher. The adequacy of the flowage easements obtained from landowners by the Corps, in advance of the intentional releases, is front and center in two pending class action complaints arising from the releases, claiming takings.[119]

Beyond flowage easement issues, the intentional-flooding litigation poses the question whether the flooding should be analyzed as a potential tort or instead as a potential Fifth Amendment taking of property rights. Here there is a climate-change-related twist. Under long-established case law, the distinction between a flood that is a tort and one that is a taking turns on whether the flooding, if not permanent, is at least "inevitably recurring."[120] If inevitably recurring, the flood is to be analyzed as a possible taking, specifically as a taking by permanent physical occupation, and jurisdiction vests in the Court of Federal Claims. If not, the flood is at most a tort and jurisdiction lies in the district court.[121] In both the Mississippi River class actions, the United

---

[115] CRS Report RL34131, *Flood Damage Related to Army Corps of Engineers Projects Selected Legal Issues*, by Cynthia Brougher.

[116] In re Katrina Canal Breaches Litigation, 2012 WL 678135 (5th Cir. March 2, 2012).

[117] Nicholson v. United States, 77 Fed. Cl. 605 (2007) (United States' failure to adequately design, build, or maintain flood protection system in New Orleans before and after Hurricane Katrina did not effect taking; rather, property damage was due to flooding caused by storm surge and such flooding was not the direct, natural, or probable result of the flood protection system).

[118] *See generally* David M. Stein, *Flood of Litigation Theories of Liability of Government Entities for Damages Resulting from Levee Breaches*, 52 Loy. L. Rev. 1335 (2006).

[119] Quebedeaux v. United States, No. 11-389L (Fed. Cl. filed September 21, 2011); Big Oak Farms, Inc. v. United States, No. 11-275L (Fed. Cl. filed September 9, 2011). *See generally* Brian Lee and Alice M. Noble-Allgire, *High Water in the Nation's Breadbasket A Takings Analysis of the Government's Response to the Mississippi River's Great Flood of 2011*, 26 Probate and Property 28 (January/February 2012).

[120] *See, e.g.*, United States v. Cress, 243 U.S. 316, 328 (1917); Arkansas Game & Fish Comm'n v. United States, 648 F.3d 1377, 1379 (Fed. Cir. 2011), *cert. granted*, 2012 Westlaw 1069212 (April 2, 2012).

[121] The question whether flooding that is not "inevitably recurring" necessarily falls short of being a taking, even a temporary taking, is now before the Supreme Court. *Arkansas Game & Fish Comm'n, supra* note 116.

States has filed motions to dismiss alleging that the rarity of intentional releases like those in the case demands that they be regarded as not "inevitably recurring," hence at best a tort. But the scientific consensus asserts that as climate change progresses, extreme precipitation events such as those at issue here may become more common. If that happens, will the United States be able to assert that future intentional releases of floodwaters following heavy precipitation are not inevitably recurring, hence are at most a tort? The distinction is of some moment, given that legal defenses available to the United States in the event of a tort are not available in the event of a taking.[122]

A final levee-related issue is suggested by a recent news article describing opposition of residents in Virginia's Middle Peninsula to planners' proposal to rezone land for use as a dike against rising water, and noting that "[o]utside of greater New Orleans, Hampton Roads is at the biggest risk from sea-level rise of any area its size in the United States."[123] Again, the spectre of takings claims looms if the rezoning results in the severe devaluation of parcels, or is analyzed as a physical taking.

E. Failure to Take Preventive Measures

The scientific consensus that climate change will lead to further sea level rise raises the issue whether governments can be held liable for failing to act to avert the harmful impacts of such rise. Generally, failure to act cannot be the basis of a taking claim. But when a city fails to act on a hazard that is specific and well understood, negligence may lie. Thus, in one case with relevance to future heavy rains from climate change, the court held that allegations that a city was aware of the potential for overflow from the city landfill's retention ponds, and its subsequent failure to take measures to prevent such overflow, did not state a taking claim, but did properly assert negligence.[124]

VI. Other Adaptation Responses to Climate Change

The previous section touched on a few adaptation measures specifically related to sea level rise. This section continues with additional adaption measures that raise legal issues.[125]

---

[122] *See* CRS Report RL34131, *Flood Damage Related to Army Corps of Engineers Projects Selected Legal Issues*, *supra* note 115. The principal tort defenses, discussed in CRS Report RL34131, *Flood Damage Related to Army Corps of Engineers Projects Selected Legal Issues*, are two—the Corps of Engineers typically asserting both in each case. First, there is §3 of the Flood Control Act of 1928, 33 U.S.C. §702c, declaring that "[n]o liability of any kind shall attach to or rest upon the United States for any damage from or by flood waters at any place ...." Second, there is the "discretionary function exemption" under the Federal Tort Claims Act (FTCA), under which no tort can be maintained against the United States if based on a federal official's "exercise or performance or the failure to exercise or perform a discretionary function." 28 U.S.C. §2680(a). This exemption from the FTCA waiver of sovereign immunity protects federal officials from liability for decisions where there is room for policy judgment and discretion, and would likely apply to Corps of Engineers decisions as to operation of the agency's facilities.

By contrast, the waiver of sovereign immunity for Fifth Amendment takings claims against the United States, found in the Tucker Act (28 U.S.C. §1491), has no comparable exemptions.

[123] Darryl Fears, "Climate change fight intensifies in Virginia," Wash. Post December 18, 2011, at A3.

[124] City of El Paso v. Ramirez, 349 S.W.3d 181 (Tex. App. 2011). *See generally* Annot., *Liability for overflow or escape of water from reservoir, ditch, or artificial pond*, 169 ALR 517.

[125] In a definitive study of possible regulatory adaptations to sea level rise, the following are listed as possible "regulatory tools": zoning and overlay zones, floodplain regulations, building codes and resilient design, (continued...)

A. Beach Issues

1. Armoring

Shoreline "armoring"—seawalls, revetments, and bulkheads[126]—has obvious relevance to climate-change-caused sea level rise. The definition of armoring in the Florida administrative code is as good as any: "a manmade structure designed to either prevent erosion of the upland property or protect eligible structures from the effects of coastal wave and current action."[127] The right to erect shore defense structures on one's property has long-standing common law imprimatur, yet the practice has its detractors. Seawalls, for example, have been said to deflect waves onto other beaches, causing sand to be scoured away, and also to cut off the natural supply of sand to the beach from the sand dune behind the wall.

Many have proposed that states adopt anti-armoring statutes, so as to allow the natural landward migration of the land-water boundary caused by sea level rise. Such natural migration of the boundary allows the creation of new, ecologically valuable wetlands to replace those lost to sea level rise, and the expansion of public trust lands. An obvious issue, however, is whether these consequences of anti-armoring laws trench on private property rights in a manner that must be compensated as a taking. Though the issue is certainly unresolved by the limited relevant litigation, the balance of arguments seems to tip against a taking. Most obviously, the harm to the littoral owner (from flooding and encroaching public trust lands) likely would be viewed by courts as resulting from sea level rise, not the armoring restriction.[128]

A taking claim was rejected, logically enough, where the shore owner proposed armoring on public trust lands. The case is *McQueen v. South Carolina Coastal Council*,[129] in which the state denied the owner of a tract along a manmade canal permission to build a seawall and to backfill. Even though without the seawall the tract was assumed to be unbuildable and have zero value, no taking of plaintiff's property was found to have occurred. As the court saw it, plaintiff's land had largely reverted to public-trust tideland belonging to the state by the time his application was denied. Thus, the seawall permission denial took nothing plaintiff had at the time of his application. Recall the earlier discussion of shifting public trust in connection with this case in section IV.A.

In the absence of armoring restrictions, one can expect sea level rise to cause more beachfront land owners to install defensive structures. As a result, questions as to liability for harm to neighboring tracts may be raised more often. A hoary common law principle, the "common

---

(...continued)

setbacks/buffers, conditional development and exactions, rebuilding restrictions, subdivisions and cluster development, hard-armoring permits, soft-armoring permits, and rolling coastal management / rolling easement statutes. Jessica Grannis, Georgetown Climate Center, *Adaptation Tool Kit, Sea-Level Rise and Coastal Land Use How Governments Can Use Land Use Practices to Adapt to Sea-Level Rise* (2011).

[126] In this report, "armoring" does not include levees erected for flood protection, though some writers would extend the term that far. Levees are treated separately in Section IV.D.

[127] Fla. Admin. Code R. 63B-33.002(5).

[128] For a fuller recitation of the takings arguments pro and con with respect to anti-armoring statutes, see J. Peter Byrne, *Rising Seas and Common Law Baselines A Comment on Regulatory Takings Discourse Concerning Climate Change*, 11 Vt. J. Envtl. L. 625, 636-638 (2010).

[129] 580 S.E.2d 116 (S.C. 2003).

enemy doctrine," holds that one may erect defenses against the sea even though doing so may cause water to beat with added force against adjoining lands and require the adjoining landowner to also erect defenses.[130] Many states, however, have moved away from the common enemy doctrine toward a rule of reasonableness, under which liability for harm to others is avoided only when the interference with the flow of surface waters is "reasonable," a term that could benefit from judicial clarification.[131]

One case takes on the tantalizing question of whether armoring structures block the landward shift of the line between public and private ownership, typically the mean high water mark, when that mark reaches such a structure. In *United States (Lummi Nation) v. Milner*,[132] the Ninth Circuit said no; the ownership line continues to move as if the armoring structure had not been built. While the upland owner has the right to erect structures on his or her property to defend against erosion and storm damage, the tideland owner has "a vested right to the ambulatory boundary and to the tidelands they would gain if the boundary were allowed to ambulate."[133] In short, the upland owner "[does] not have the right to permanently fix the property boundary" absent the tideland owner's consent.[134] The court pointed out that its ruling might have limited applicability, given that the tideland owner here was an Indian tribe and its federal trustee, rather than the state as in the usual case. This allowed the federal court to create federal common law, while most such disputes over tideland/upland boundaries are handled by state courts under state law. One commentator notes that "[t]he decision, if applied generally, might make many homes now behind seawalls trespassers on state property."[135]

2. Renourishment

Adding sand back to eroded beaches or building up beaches, often called beach "nourishment" or "renourishment," may be increasingly resorted to as climate change progresses and sea level rises. In the near term (but unlikely beyond), repairing the ravages of storms may be preferable to the difficulties of moving existing coastal population inland. Even Members of Congress who generally seek to limit federal spending have strongly supported Corps of Engineers beach restoration projects where the local economy depends on attractive beaches.[136]

The Supreme Court, too, has turned its attention recently to beach renourishment projects. In *Stop the Beach Renourishment, Inc. v. Florida Dep't of Environmental Protection*,[137] the Court confronted a Florida beach renourishment project that had sparked objections from a handful of the affected beachfront property owners. Those owners insisted that by adding a strip of state-owned beach in front of their eroded privately owned beach, the state had effected a Fifth

---

[130] United States (Lummi Nation) v. Milner, 583 F.3d 1174, 1189 (9th Cir. 2009), *citing* Revell v. People, 52 N.E. 1052, 1059 (Ill. 1898).

[131] *See generally* Wendy B. Davis, *Reasonable Use Has Become the Common Enemy*, 9 Alb. L. Envtl. Outlook J. 1, 9-10 (2004).

[132] 583 F.3d 1174 (9th Cir. 2009).

[133] *Id.* at 1189-1190.

[134] *Id.* at 1190.

[135] Joe Sax, *Some Unorthodox Thoughts About Rising Sea Levels, Beach Erosion, and Property Rights*, 11 Vt. J. Envtl. L. 641, 642 n.7 (2010).

[136] Evan Lehmann, *Conservative lawmakers, protecting their beaches, also adapt to climate change* (E&E Climatewire February 10, 2012).

[137] 130 S. Ct. 2592 (2011).

Amendment taking of two of their littoral property rights: the right to ownership of future accreted land and the right to direct contact with the water. The Supreme Court held unanimously that the Florida Supreme Court had properly found no taking, since the shore owners had not shown that these littoral rights were superior to the state's right to fill in its submerged land. Note that the restored beach belonged to the state: "Florida law as it stood before the decision below allowed the state to fill in its own seabed, and the resulting sudden exposure of previously submerged land was treated like an avulsion for purposes of ownership."[138] Avulsions, recall, do not move ownership boundaries.

While *Stop the Beach Renourishment* was a victory for beach renourishment efforts, the decision turned on Florida case law precedent that may not be replicated in other states. Thus, legal challenges by littoral owners to beach restoration projects can be expected to continue.

Because the Florida and U.S. supreme courts found no property rights impaired in *Stop the Beach Renourishment*, they had no occasion to clarify how the *benefit* to the beachfront property owner from renourishment might factor into the taking analysis. This is a pivotal question if the costs of beach renourishment are to remain affordable, but two recent state court decisions give opposite answers. In one, a New Jersey court confronted a municipality's condemnation of an easement to erect a 22-foot-high dune on beachfront property, to protect the barrier island from storms.[139] The court held that the jury's $375,000 compensation award, largely for the dune's partial blockage of the ocean view, was not to be reduced by the storm-protection benefit conferred on the property owner. Under well-established law, the court said, compensation awarded a condemnee is offset only by benefits of the project specific to the condemnee ("special benefits"), not those enjoyed by the community at large ("general benefits"). The benefit conferred by the dune was protection of the island from storms—in the court's view, a general benefit, hence not an offset. A contrary view comes from a North Carolina court in a case where a state agency offered zero compensation for an easement over private beachfront property needed to implement a beach renourishment project. The court found the offer reasonable (though subject to final determination in an eminent domain proceeding), citing the renourishment project's benefits to the beachfront property owner as adequate compensation.[140]

B. "Retreat" — moving development inland

Levees, armoring, and beach restoration, discussed above, have long been well-understood techniques, widely supported by land owners if not by environmentalists. Given sea level rise of the magnitude predicted in connection with climate change, however, the long-term viability of such structural protections seems dubious.[141] Attention is shifting instead toward "retreat"—an unfortunately pejorative term denoting government actions that discourage new development in disaster-prone areas (proactive retreat) or reconstruction following such disasters (reactive retreat).[142] When that discouragement takes the form of outright regulatory prohibition—rather than merely removal of development incentives—the taking issue is likely to arise yet again.[143]

---

[138] *Id.* at 2611.

[139] Borough of Harvey Cedars v. Karan, 40 A.3d 75 (N.J. Super. App. Div.), *certification granted* (June 8, 2012).

[140] Fisher v. Town of Nags Head, 725 S.E.2d 99 (N.C. Ct. App. 2012).

[141] The opening paragraphs of this section draw their inspiration from *Coastal Retreat Measures*, *supra* note 106.

[142] Thus far, reactive retreat appears to be the more common, but the pattern may be shifting. For example, the Oregon Coastal Management Program recently recommended "using land-use planning processes to address climate change." (continued...)

The legal question is whether the specific context of sea level rise due to climate change may offer the government defenses against regulatory takings claims not otherwise available. One possible starting point is *Lucas v. South Carolina Coastal Council.*[144] There, the Supreme Court dealt with a state beachfront management act aimed in large part at protecting the beach/dune system along the state's coast. Toward that end, the act sought to "discourage[e] new construction in close proximity to the beach/dune system and encourag[e] those who have erected structures too close to the system to retreat from it."[145] In particular, the plaintiff was barred from building any occupiable structure on his two beachfront lots. The Court pointedly rejected the state's assertion that the statute, by asserting avoidance of a public harm as its purpose, was immunized from takings liability. Only state action based on "background principles of the State's law of property and nuisance" was so protected,[146] said the Court, holding that the beachfront management act did not fall into that category. Traditional common law, it observed, rarely supports prohibiting the erection of a house.[147]

Lucas suggests that the possibility that a tract of land will be submerged in the future as the result of climate change may not be sufficient to deflect takings or other legal challenges against a development prohibition on that tract—at least when, as in *Lucas*, the prohibition eliminates all land value. In *Lucas*, not even the fact that plaintiff's lots had been submerged at various times in the previous 40 years was enough to shield the state from takings liability. And while public trust doctrine has been held to be a "background principle" immunizing the state,[148] there is no support for any extension of public trust doctrine, as a defense to takings claims, to lands not below the mean high water mark when the development prohibition is imposed. Arguably, however, the question remains open.[149]

The *Lucas* decision, rendered in 1992, did not consider climate change. And because *Lucas* dealt with a "total taking"—that is, a regulatory restriction eliminating *all* use and value in a tract of land—it did not deal with takings law factors confined to *less-than-total* elimination of use and value. One such factor is the extent to which the government action interfered with the landowner's "reasonable investment-backed expectations" (RIBEs).

(...continued)

Oregon Coastal Management Program, Department of Land Conservation and Development, *Climate Ready Communities A Strategy for Adapting to the Impacts of Climate Change on the Oregon Coast* at 5 (January 2009). And a Hawaii state representative has introduced legislation requiring her state and its counties to acknowledge climate change in any future development taking place on the islands. *Bill requires Hawaii to prepare for sea level rise* (E&E ClimateWire January 26, 2012).

[143] As the text notes, in contrast with regulatory prohibitions the mere removal of government development incentives is unlikely to be held a taking. *See, e.g.,* Texas Landowners Rights Ass'n v, Harris, 453 F. Supp. 1025 (D.D.C. 1978), *aff'd mem.,* 598 F.2d 311 (D.C. Cir. 1979), in connection with the National Flood Insurance Program. Another incentive-removing federal statute, the Coastal Barrier Resources Act, ended federal support (such as federal mortgage guarantees and federal flood insurance) for development on certain barrier islands. 16 U.S.C. §§3501-3510. It has generated no reported takings decisions.

[144] 505 U.S. 1003 (1992).

[145] *Id.* at 1021 n.10.

[146] *Id.* at 1029.

[147] *Id.* at 1031.

[148] *See, e.g.,* McQueen v. South Carolina Coastal Council, 580 S.E.2d 116, 119 n.5 (S.C. 2003).

[149] *See* F. Patrick Hubbard, *The Impact of Lucas on Coastal Development Background Principles, the Public Trust Doctrine and Global Warming,* 16 Southeastern Envtl. L. J. 65, 80 (2007).

The RIBEs question here revolves around recent or future purchasers of land prone to climate-change-induced extreme weather, such as flooding. Can such purchasers be charged with constructive knowledge of the scientific consensus that climate change will bring about more frequent instances of extreme weather in the future? Can such purchasers, as a result, be held "on notice" that state or local governments might restrict development of such parcels in the future, weakening any claim that such restrictions interfere with *reasonable* expectations of development when the land was acquired? Would the existence of a widely publicized government retreat proposal at the time when the land was acquired strengthen an on-notice/absence-of-RIBEs argument by the government? And could states bolster this defense by requiring that all purchasers of disaster-prone land be given written notice prior to purchase of the risks to which they were exposing themselves?[150] Even today, "[s]everal [state] disclosure statutes require inclusion of whether the property has been affected by floods or is in a flood zone or plain."[151] The extremely thin case law on whether such notice undercuts a taking claim based on development restrictions points to notice not making much difference.[152] But it is far too early to regard the matter as settled.

The question has also been raised whether local jurisdictions might be successfully sued in the opposite situation—that is, where they *fail* to restrict development despite having knowledge that flooding may occur, following which the permitted development is damaged by flooding or exacerbates flooding on other properties.[153]

Further inland, the National Flood Insurance Program (NFIP) becomes a central player in discouraging construction in flood-prone areas[154]—floods that in some instances may become more severe or frequent as the result of climate change-related sea level rise or extreme rainfall. A local jurisdiction's participation in the NFIP is voluntary. It is embodied in an agreement under which the community adopts floodplain management ordinances meeting minimum NFIP requirements for regulating new-construction design in "special flood hazard areas,"[155] and use restrictions in the regulatory floodway. In return, the federal government makes subsidized federal flood insurance available to landowners in those jurisdictions.

Courts have unanimously rejected takings suits based on NFIP-inspired floodplain ordinances, or similar non-NFIP floodplain ordinances.[156] Should future sea level rise lead to stricter federal

---

[150] One commentator would answer yes to both the footnoted text question, involving written notice, and the immediately preceding text questions, involving only constructive knowledge. He argues that "increasing awareness of [sea level rise] and its impacts as well as distribution of such information should inform analysis of coastal owners' RIBE in legal claims that government regulation or action has taken private property." Thomas Ruppert, *Reasonable Investment-Backed Expectations Should Notice of Rising Seas Lead to Falling Expectations for Coastal Property Purchasers?*, 26 J. Land Use & Envtl. L. 239 (2011).

[151] *Id.* at 260, citing as an example Cal. Civ. Code §1103(v)(1)(A).

[152] *Id.* at 266-267.

[153] *See generally* James Wilkins, *Is Sea Level Rise "Foreseeable"? Does It Matter?*, 26 Vt. J. Envtl L. 437 (2011).

[154] 42 U.S.C. §§4001-4128.

[155] Special flood hazard areas are mapped by the Federal Emergency Management Agency, which administers the NFIP generally. 44 C.F.R. §59.2(b).

[156] *See, e.g.*, Adolph v. Federal Emergency Management Agency, 854 F.2d 732 (5th Cir. 1988); Gove v. Zoning Bd. Of Appeals, 831 N.E.2d 865, 871-875 (Mass. 2005); Responsible Citizens in Opposition to Floodplain Ordinance v. City of Asheville, 302 S.E.2d 204 (N.C. 1983). *But see* McDougal v. County of Imperial, 942 F.2d 668 (9th Cir. 1991) (fact that government's purpose in floodway designation was legitimate does not automatically preclude regulatory takings claim).

---

conditions for flood insurance in the form of stricter floodplain ordinances, takings issues inevitably will rear their head once more. A recent change in the law, directing the NFIP to consider future sea level rise and not just historical flood data in creating floodplain maps, could provide additional basis for such stricter requirements.[157] One can expect, however, that the current judicial refusal to impute to the United States any takings liability for such local ordinances will continue to stand as long as their adoption remains voluntary.[158]

Finally, local jurisdictions have asked whether their potential disinvestment in public infrastructure in low-lying areas (such as armoring, roads, and wastewater treatment plants) might raise takings issues.[159] The aim of such disinvestment would be to hold down flood-induced costs by discouraging new development in such areas or stimulating removal of existing development. Affected property owners, however, may not be so civic-minded. For example, a state's decision to discontinue maintenance of a shoreside road that is eroding away might lead those dependent on that road for access to their property to assert a taking by denial of access.[160] The viability of such takings claims will vary widely with the facts. No reported takings decisions at all exist in response to the federal government's disinvestment in the development of coastal barrier islands through the Coastal Barrier Resources Act.[161] On the other hand, disinvestment in public infrastructure may be dicier if the courts perceive a state or local government duty to maintain existing infrastructure.[162] Presumably, takings problems can be lessened by announcing disinvestment many years (even a decade or more) in advance; such "amortization periods" have been effective in other factual contexts, such as billboard removal programs, in deflecting takings claims.[163] Governments might also take care not to allow disinvestment in an area to get too far ahead of the retreat activity of those living and working there.

---

[157] P.L. 112-141, Div. F, tit. II, subtit. A (Biggert-Waters Flood Insurance Reform Act of 2012) §§ 100215(d)(1), 100216(b)(3)(D).

[158] *Adolph*, 854 F.2d 732 (holding that Federal Emergency Management Agency cannot be sued for taking based on parish's adoption of floodplain regulations to qualify for NFIP, because adoption was not federally coerced).

[159] This paragraph discussing disinvestment in public infrastructure was inspired by David Lewis, *Constitutional Property Law Analysis of State and Local Government Disinvestment in Infrastructure as a Coastal Adaptation Strategy* (2012) (student paper on file with author).

[160] *See, e.g.,* Jordan v. Canton, 265 A.2d 96 (Me. 1970).

[161] 16 U.S.C. §§3501-3510.

[162] *See, e.g.,* Jordan v. St. Johns County, 63 So. 3d 835 (Fla. App. 2011) (argument that county has so failed in its duty to maintain road as to deprive property owner of access states taking claim; government inaction in the face of an affirmative duty to act can support taking claim).

[163] "Amortization programs dovetail nicely with the traditional notion of land-use planning that nonconforming uses should be phased out gradually rather than terminated immediately." R. Meltz, D.H. Merriam, and R.M. Frank, THE TAKINGS ISSUE 433 (Island Press 1999). The value of an amortization period for avoiding takings is well-established. *See, e.g.,* Naegele Outdoor Advertising Co. v. City of Durham, 844 F.2d 172, 177 (4th Cir. 1988).

VII. Responding To and Rebuilding After Natural Disasters

A. Responding

Legal questions inevitably arise as to whether public and private actions taken in an emergency, climate-change-related or otherwise, are subject to the same legal requirements as when there is no emergency. And, for that matter, what constitutes an emergency—a term generally left undefined in statutes. There is no explicit, across-the-board exemption in any federal environmental law for emergency response.

A sampler of less-than-across-the-board provisions reflecting the need for expedition in emergencies might include, first, the Superfund Act.[164] Under this act, government response to releases or threatened releases of hazardous substances, as when a flood jeopardizes containment of hazardous chemicals at a site, can be done hurriedly as emergency actions (known as "removal actions") with less prior study and investigation than is required for permanent cleanups (known as "remedial actions"). Similarly, Council on Environmental Quality regulations implementing the National Environmental Policy Act (NEPA) say that where emergency circumstances require a federal agency to take action without observing the regulations, the agency should consult with the Council about "alternative arrangements."[165] Federal actions not needed to control the immediate impacts of the emergency, however, remain fully subject to NEPA review.

B. Rebuilding

Following a natural calamity in which structures are destroyed, questions often arise whether the rebuilding of a structure essentially as it was before, in the very same location, is subject to the full range of environmental and other requirements applicable if the structure were being built there for the first time. Here, besides the question of what constitutes an emergency, there is the added issue whether the replacement structure is essentially the same as its predecessor (changes are always made to some degree). As with responding to emergencies (previous section), there appears to be no explicit, across-the-board exemption in federal environmental law.

Probably the broadest exemption in federal statutes for rebuilding structures is that in the Stafford Disaster Relief Act. The act decrees that no environmental impact statement (EIS) under NEPA is required for "[a]n action which is taken or assistance which is provided pursuant to [the Act], which has the effect of restoring a facility substantially to its condition prior to the disaster or emergency."[166] Also as to NEPA, Department of Transportation regulations allow for categorical exclusions from EIS preparation for reconstruction (whether prompted by a disaster or not) of highways, bridges, and rail and bus facilities.[167] Limited NEPA case law on the replacement issue

---

[164] 42 U.S.C. §§9601-9675.

[165] 40 C.F.R. §1506 11. See also the NEPA regulations of the Corps of Engineers, which call on that agency, in responding to emergencies, to refer actions with potentially significant environmental impacts to the CEQ as to NEPA arrangements "[w]hen possible." 33 C.F.R. §230.8.

[166] 42 U.S.C. §5159.

[167] 23 C.F.R. §771.117(d).

indicates that federal involvement in the construction of an essentially similar replacement facility does not require an EIS—as long as the environment *with* the original facility is accepted as the status quo baseline.[168] This qualifier suggests that the passage of several years before the new facility is built, accompanied by a change in the environment at the site, might cause the *changed* environment to be viewed as the baseline. With the changed environment as the baseline, the federal action might be seen as having significant impact, triggering the EIS requirement.

Outside of NEPA, the Clean Water Act affords an exemption from its requirement of permits for the discharge of dredged or fill material "for the purpose of emergency reconstruction ... of currently serviceable structures such as dikes, dams, levees, ... and transportation structures."[169] Also, three nationwide permits issued by the Corps of Engineers under this permit program cover reconstruction in varying degrees, relieving the applicant of the more expensive and time-consuming process of applying for an individual permit.[170]

VIII. Immigration and Refugee Law[171]

United Nations High Commissioner for Refugees Antonio Guterres has said: "Climate change is today one of the main drivers of forced displacement, both directly through impact on environment—not allowing people to live any more in the areas where they were traditionally living—and as a trigger of extreme poverty and conflict."[172] Climate-related migrants, however, are not considered a "protected class" of people in international law or U.S. immigration law, nor is there a specific legal framework or entity responsible for their displacement.

In international law, the foundational document is the 1951 Convention Relating to the Status of Refugees, which defines "refugee" as a person with a "well-founded fear of being persecuted for reasons of race, religion, nationality, membership of a particular social group, or political opinion"[173]—unlikely, it would seem, to embrace climate change refugees. Similarly, the United States has long held to the principle that it will not return a foreign national to a country where his life or freedom would be threatened, but this principle does not encompass economic or environmental migrants. The Immigration and Nationality Act (INA) requires foreign nationals seeking asylum or refugee status to demonstrate a well-founded fear that, if returned home, they

---

[168] Sierra Club v. Hassell, 636 F.2d 1095, 1099 (5th Cir. 1981) (replacement of bridge destroyed by hurricane requires no EIS). *Accord*, Citizens for the Scenic Severn River Bridge, Inc. v. Skinner, 802 F. Supp. 1325, 1333 (D. Md. 1991).

[169] 33 U.S.C. §1344(f)(1)(B).

[170] *See* Nationwide Permit No. 3 (repair, rehabilitation, or replacement of any previously authorized, currently serviceable structure), No. 31 (maintenance of existing flood control facilities), and No. 45 (restoration of upland areas damaged by storms, floods, or other discrete events, including bank stabilization). 77 Fed. Reg. 10,270 (February 21, 2012).

[171] This section of the report was written by Ruth Wasem, Specialist in Immigration Policy, CRS Domestic Social Policy Division.

[172] "Conflicts Fuelled by Climate Change Causing New Refugee Crisis, Warns UN," by Julian Borger, *The Guardian*, (June 17, 2008), available online at: http://www.guardian.co.uk/environment/2008/jun/17/climatechange.food. See *also* United Nations High Commissioner on Refugees, THE STATE OF THE WORLD'S REFUGEES 2012: IN SEARCH OF SOLIDARITY ch. 7 ("Displacement, Climate Change, and Natural Disasters"), summary available at http://www.unhcr.org/publications/unhcr/sowr2012.

[173] The United States is not a party to the 1951 Convention but is a party to the 1967 Protocol Relating to the Status of Refugees, which amends the Convention. 19 U.S. Treaties 6223.

---

will be persecuted based upon the five characteristics listed in the Convention (above).[174] Provisions also exist in the INA to offer temporary protected status (TPS) or relief from removal when natural disasters occur or when violence and civil unrest erupt in spots around the world. While TPS may benefit people stranded in the United States because of natural disasters, it is only short-term relief from removal.[175]

Author Contact Information

Robert Meltz
Legislative Attorney
rmeltz@crs.loc.gov, 7-7891

---

[174] *See* definition of "refugee" in INA §101(a)(42), 8 U.S.C. §1101(a)(42). This definition governs the reach of INA §207, 8 U.S.C. §1157, governing admissions based on humanitarian concerns, and INA §208, 8 U.S.C. §1158, governing asylum.

[175] For further background, see CRS Report RL31269, *Refugee Admissions and Resettlement Policy*, by Andorra Bruno; CRS Report R41753, *Asylum and "Credible Fear" Issues in U.S. Immigration Policy*, by Ruth Ellen Wasem; and CRS Report RS20844, *Temporary Protected Status Current Immigration Policy and Issues*, by Ruth Ellen Wasem and Karma Ester.
